disc one

disc two

insert disc one

You Gotta Sing

You gotta sing when your spirit says sing,
You gotta sing when your spirit says sing,
When your spirit says sing,
you gotta **sing right along**,
You gotta sing when your spirit says sing.

You gotta shout when your spirit says shout,
You gotta shout when your spirit says shout,
When your spirit says shout,
you gotta **shout right out loud**,
You gotta shout when your spirit says shout.

You gotta wiggle when your spirit says wiggle,
You gotta wiggle when your spirit says wiggle,
When your spirit says wiggle,
you gotta **wiggle like a worm**,
You gotta wiggle when your spirit says wiggle.

You gotta shake when your spirit says shake,
You gotta shake when your spirit says shake,
When your spirit says shake,
        you gotta shake like a snake,
You gotta shake when your spirit says shake.

You gotta dance when your spirit says dance,
You gotta dance when your spirit says dance,
When your spirit says dance,
        you gotta dance right along,
You gotta dance when your spirit says dance.

        (Let's dance!)

You gotta sing when your spirit says sing,
You gotta sing when your spirit says sing,
When your spirit says sing,
        you gotta sing right along,
You gotta sing when your spirit says sing,
You gotta sing when your spirit says sing.

You gotta stop when your spirit says stop.

Traditional. Adapted by Nancy Cassidy © 1988

Wabash cannonball

Whoo! Whoo!

From the **wide** Pacific Ocean
to the broad Atlantic **shore**,

She climbs the flowery **mountains**
over **hills** and by the shore,

Although she's **tall** and handsome,
she's known quite well by **all**,

She's a regular combination,
the **Wabash Cannonball**.

CHORUS

Oh, listen to the jingle,
to the rumble and the roar,

As she flies along the woodlands,
over hills and by the shore,

Hear the mighty rush of the engine,
hear the merry hobo's squall,

As she rumbles through the
jungles, the Wabash Cannonball.

Whoo! Whoo!
Whoo! Whoo!

Now the eastern states are **dandy**
so the western **people** say,
From New York to St. Louis, Chicago, **by the way,**
Through the **hills** of Minnesota where the rippling **waters fall,**
No chances to be taken on the **Wabash Cannonball**.

Back to the chorus

Whoo! Whoo!
Whoo! Whoo!
Whoo! Whoo!
Whoo! Whoo!

Traditional

CD 1/TRACK 2

7

Day-o

CHORUS
Day-o, me say day-o,

Daylight come and me wanna go home,

Day-o, me say day-o,

Daylight come and me wanna go home.

Work all night 'til the mornin' come,

Daylight come and me wanna go home,
Stack banana 'til the mornin' come,
Daylight come and me wanna go home.

Come mister tallyman, tally me banana,
Daylight come and me wanna go home,
Come mister tallyman, tally me banana,
Daylight come and me wanna go home.
Back to the chorus

A beautiful bunch o' ripe banana,
Daylight come and me wanna go home,
Lift six hand, seven hand, eight hand bunch,
Daylight come and me wanna go home.

Come mister tallyman, tally me banana,
Daylight come and me wanna go home,
Come mister tallyman, tally me banana,
Daylight come and me wanna go home.
Back to the chorus

Day-o, me say day-o,

Daylight come and me wanna go home.

Traditional
CD 1/TRACK 3

TING-A-LAY-o

hee! haw!
hee! haw!

CHORUS
TING-A-LAY-o,
run my little donkey, run,
TING-A-LAY-o,
run my little donkey, run.

My donkey **hee**, my donkey **haw**,
My donkey **sleep in a bed of straw**,
My donkey **short**, my donkey **wide**,
Don't get too **close to his back side**.
Back to the chorus

hee! haw!

My donkey **walk**, my donkey **talk**,
My donkey **eats with a knife and fork**,
My donkey **eat**, my donkey **sleep**,
My donkey **kicks** with his
two hind feet.
Back to the chorus

boo hoo!

My donkey **laugh**, my donkey **cry**,
My donkey **love peanut butter pie**,
My donkey **laugh**, my donkey **cry**,
My donkey **love peanut butter pie**.
Back to the chorus, repeat twice

Ting-a-lay-o, run my little donkey, run,
Ting-a-lay-o, run my little donkey, run.

Traditional

CD 1/TRACK 4

mister Sun

Oh, Mister Sun, Sun,
Mister Golden Sun,
Please shine down on me.

Oh, Mister Sun, Sun,
Mister Golden Sun,
Hiding behind a tree.

These little children are asking you,
To please come out so we can play with you.
Oh, Mister Sun, Sun, Mister Golden Sun,
Please shine down on me.

Oh, Mister Moon, Moon,
bright and silvery moon,
Please shine down on me.

Oh, Mister Moon, Moon,
bright and silvery moon,
come from behind that tree.

I like to ramble, and I like to roam,
But I like to find myself at home.
When the moon, moon,
bright and silvery moon,
Comes shining down on me.

These little children
are asking you,
To please come out so we can play with you.
Oh, Mister Sun, Sun, Mister Golden Sun,
Please shine down on, won't you shine
down on, please shine down on me.

Traditional. Adapted by Nancy Cassidy © 1988

CD 1/ TRACK 5

Father's old grey

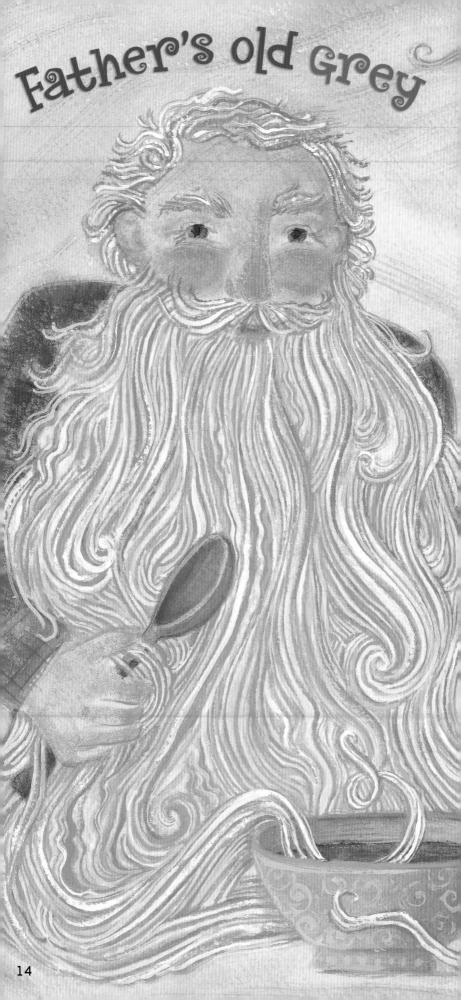

14

Whiskers

I have a **dear old daddy**,
For whom I nightly pray,
He has a **set of whiskers**,
That are always in the way.

CHORUS
They're always in the way,
The cows eat them for hay,
They hide the dirt on Daddy's shirt,
They're always in the way.

Around the supper table,
We make a **happy group**,
Until dear Father's whiskers,
Get **tangled in the soup**.
Back to the Chorus

Father had a strong back,
But now it's **all caved in**,
He stepped upon his whiskers,
And **walked up to his chin**.
Back to the Chorus

We have a **dear old mother**,
With him at night she sleeps,
She wakes up in the morning,
Eating shredded wheat.
Back to the Chorus, repeat twice

Traditional

CD 1/TRACK 6

Baby Beluga

Baby Beluga in the deep blue sea,
Swim so wild and you swim so free.
Heaven above, and the sea below,
And a little white whale on the go.

Baby Beluga, Baby Beluga,
Is the water warm?
Is your mama home, with you, so happy?

Way down yonder where the dolphins play,
Where you dive and splash all day.
Waves roll in and the waves roll out,
See the water squirtin' out of your spout.

Baby Beluga, Baby Beluga,
Sing your little song, Sing for all your friends,
We like to hear you.

When it's dark, and you're home and fed,
Curl up snug in your water bed.
Moon is shining and the stars are out,
Good night, little whale, good night.

Baby Beluga, Baby Beluga,
With tomorrow's sun, another day's begun,
You'll soon be waking.

Baby Beluga in the deep blue sea,
Swim so wild and swim so free.
Heaven above and the sea below,
And a little white whale on the go.
You're just a little white whale on the go.

Words by Raffi, D. Pike. Music by Raffi. © 1980 Homeland
Publishing (SOCAN), a division of Troubadour Music Inc.
All rights reserved. Used by permission.

CD 1/TRACK 7

17

Willoughby Wallaby Woo

Willoughby, wallaby woo,
An elephant sat on you!

Willoughby, wallaby wee,
An elephant sat on me!

1 Willoughby, wallaby **webecca**,
An elephant sat on **Rebecca**!

2 Willoughby, wallaby **warlie**,
An elephant sat on **Charlie**!

3 Willoughby, wallaby **wam**,
An elephant sat on **Sam**!

4 Willoughby, wallaby **wusan**,
An elephant sat on **Susan**!

I hope that you sing along, Sing along, along with me.

5. Rosa...	9. Justin...	13. Leslie...
6. Carlos...	10. Sally...	14. Mark...
7. Robin...	11. Eric...	15. Nancy...
8. Scott...	12. John...	All of us!

*Based on a poem by Dennis Lee © 1974 by Dennis Lee
From "Alligator Pie" with permission of the MacMillan
Company of Canada Limited. Music by Larry Miyata.
Adapted lyrics by Raffi © Copyright 1976
Homeland Publishing (CAPAC)*

CD 1/TRACK 8

18

Kumbaya

kum-ba-ya, my Lord, kum-ba-ya,
kum-ba-ya, my Lord, kum-ba-ya,

kum-ba-ya, my Lord, kum-ba-ya,
oh, Lord, kum-ba-ya.

3 Someone's dancing Lord, kum-ba-ya,
Someone's dancing Lord, kum-ba-ya,
Someone's dancing Lord, kum-ba-ya,
Oh, Lord, kum-ba-ya.

1 Someone's singing Lord, kum-ba-ya,
Someone's singing Lord, kum-ba-ya,
Someone's singing Lord, kum-ba-ya,
Oh, Lord, kum-ba-ya.

2 Someone's crying Lord, kum-ba-ya,
Someone's crying Lord, kum-ba-ya,
Someone's crying Lord, kum-ba-ya,
Oh, Lord, kum-ba-ya.

4 Come by here, my Lord, kum-ba-ya,
Come by here, my Lord, kum-ba-ya,
Come by here, my Lord, kum-ba-ya,
Oh, Lord, kum-ba-ya.

Traditional. Adapted by Nancy Cassidy © 1986

CD 1/TRACK 9

Shake my Sillies out

I'm gonna shake, shake, shake
my sillies out,
Shake, shake, shake
my sillies out,
Shake, shake, shake
my sillies out,
And wiggle my
waggles away.

I'm gonna clap, clap, clap,
my crazies out,
Clap, clap, clap
my crazies out,
Clap, clap, clap
my crazies out,
And wiggle my
waggles away.

I'm gonna jump, jump, jump
my jiggles out,
Jump, jump, jump
my jiggles out,
Jump, jump, jump
my jiggles out,
And wiggle my waggles away.

I'm gonna yawn,
yawn, yawn
my sleepies out,
Yawn, yawn, yawn
my sleepies out,
Yawn, yawn, yawn
my sleepies out,
And wiggle my
waggles away.

I'm gonna stretch, stretch,
stretch my stretchies out,
Stretch, stretch, stretch
my stretchies out,
Stretch, stretch, stretch
my stretchies out,
And wiggle my
waggles away.

I'm gonna shake, shake,
shake my sillies out,
Shake, shake, shake
my sillies out,
Shake, shake, shake
my sillies out,
And wiggle my
waggles away.

And wiggle my waggles away.

CD 1/TRACK 10

Brush your teeth

1 When you wake up in the morning
and it's quarter to ONE,
And you want to have a little fun.

You brush your teeth,
You brush your teeth.

2 When you wake up in the morning
and it's quarter to Two,
And you don't know what to do.
Back to the chorus

3 When you wake up in the morning
and it's quarter to THREE,
You've got a great big smile for me.
Back to the chorus

4 When you wake up in the morning
and it's quarter to FOUR,
You hear a great big knock
on the door.
Back to the chorus

5 When you wake up in the morning
and it's quarter to FIVE,
You're so happy to be alive.
Back to the chorus, repeat three times

Traditional. Adapted by Nancy Cassidy © 1986

CD 1/TRACK 11

Down by the Bay

 **CHORUS**
Down by the bay,
where the watermelons grow,
Back to my home, I dare not go,
for if I do, my mother will say...

Did you ever see a goose,
kissing a moose, Down by the bay?
Back to the chorus

Did you ever see a whale, with a
polka dot tail, Down by the bay?
Back to the chorus

Did you ever see a fly,
wearing a tie, Down by the bay?
Back to the chorus

Did you ever see **a bear**, **combing his hair**,
Down by the bay?
Back to the chorus

Did you ever see **llamas**, **eating their pajamas**,
Down by the bay?
Back to the chorus

Did you ever see **an octopus**,
dancing with a platypus, Down by the bay?
Back to the chorus

Did you ever **have a time**, **when you couldn't
make a rhyme**, Down by the bay? **Hey!**

Traditional. Adapted by Nancy Cassidy © 1986

CD 1/TRACK 12

Jamaica Farewell

Down the way where the nights are gay,
And the sun shines brightly on the mountain top,
I took a trip on a sailing ship,
And when I reached Jamaica, I made a stop.

CHORUS
But I'm sad to say, I'm on my way,
I won't be back for many a day,

My heart is down, my head is turning around,
I miss all my friends in Kingston town.

Down at the market you can hear,
All the ladies cry out while on their
heads they bear,
Akie rice, salt fish are nice,
And the sun is fine any time of the year.
Back to the chorus

Sounds of laughter everywhere,
And the children sway to and fro,
I must declare that my heart is there,
Though I've been from Maine to Mexico.
Back to the chorus, repeat twice

Traditional. Adapted by Nancy Cassidy © 1986

CD 1/TRACK 13

Apples and Bananas

I like to eat, eat, eat,
Apples and bananas.
I like to eat, eat, eat,
Apples and bananas.

I like to ate, ate, ate,
Ape-puls and ba-nay-nays,
I like to ate, ate, ate,
Ape-puls and ba-nay-nays.

I like to eat, eat, eat,
Ee-puls and bee-nee-nees.
I like to eat, eat, eat,
Ee-puls and bee-nee-nees.

I like to ite, ite, ite, I-puls and bi-ni-nis.
I like to ite, ite, ite, I-puls and bi-ni-nis.

I like to oat, oat, oat, O-puls and bo-no-nos.
I like to oat, oat, oat, O-puls and bo-no-nos.

I like to oot, oot, oot, Oo-puls and boo-noo-noos.
I like to oot, oot, oot, Oo-puls and boo-noo-noos.

I like to eat, eat, eat, Apples and bananas.
I like to eat, eat, eat, Apples and bananas.

Traditional

CD 1/TRACK 14

30

chicken Lips and

CHORUS
Oh, Chicken lips and lizard hips and alligator eyes,

Monkey legs, buzzard eggs
and salamander thighs,

Rabbit ears and camel rears
and tasty toenail pies,

Stir them all together, it's Mama's Soup Surprise.

**Oh, when I was a little kid
I never liked to eat,**

Mama'd put things on my plate,
I'd dump them on her feet.

But then one day she made this soup,
I ate it all in bed,

I asked her what she put in it,
and this is what she said:

Back to the chorus

Lizard Hips

I went into the bathroom
and I stood beside the sink,

I said I'm feeling slightly ill,
I think I'd like a drink,

**Mama said "I've just the thing,
I'll get it in a wink**,

It's full of lots of protein,
and vitamins, I think."

Back to the chorus, repeat last line twice

*Cody Cassidy. Words and music by John
and Nancy Cassidy © 1986 Nancy Cassidy*

CD 1/TRACK 15

It's a surprise!

Polly Wolly Doodle

Oh, I went down South for to see my gal,
Sing **polly wolly doodle** all the day,
My Sally she is a spunky gal,
Sing **polly wolly doodle** all the day.

CHORUS
Fare thee well, fare thee well,
Fare thee well, my fairy fay,
For I'm goin' to Louisiana,
For to see my Suzyanna,
Sing polly wolly doodle all the day.

Oh, a grasshopper sittin' on a railroad track,
Sing **polly wolly doodle** all the day,
A-pickin' his teeth with a carpet tack,
Sing **polly wolly doodle** all the day.
Back to the Chorus

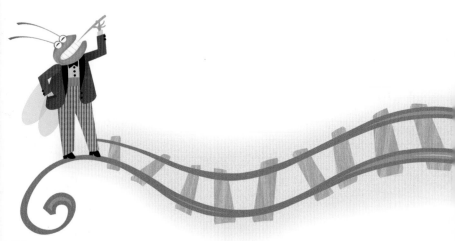

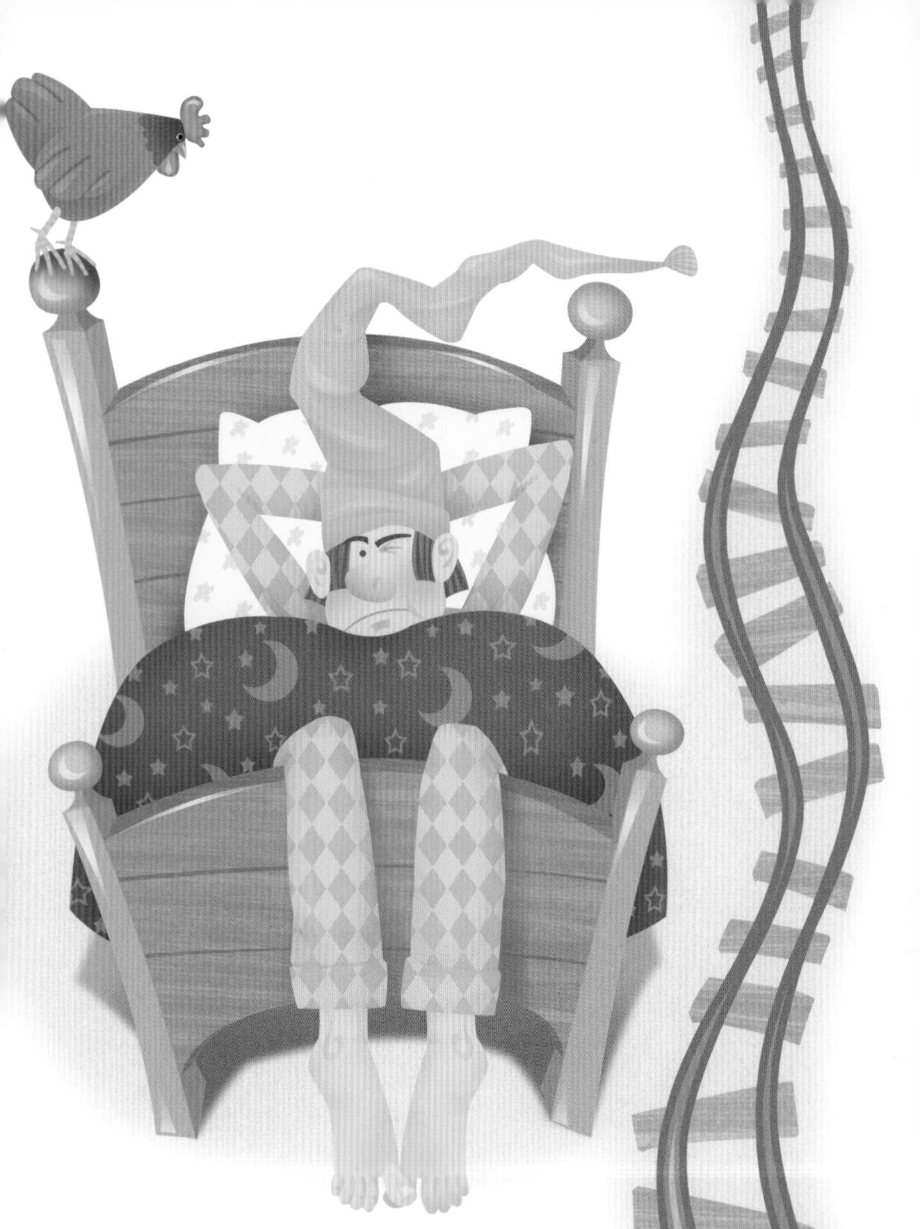

Oh, I went to bed, but it wasn't no use,
Sing **polly wolly doodle** all the day,
My feet stuck out like a chicken roost,
Sing **polly wolly doodle** all the day.
Back to the chorus

Traditional

CD 1/TRACK 16

1 This old man, he played ONE,
He played nick-nack on my thumb,
With a nick-nack-paddy-wack,
Give the dog a bone,
This old man came rolling home.

2 This old man, he played Two,
He played nick-nack on my shoe,
With a nick-nack-paddy-wack,
Give the dog a bone,
This old man came rolling home.

This old man

3 This old man, he played THREE,
He played nick-nack on my knee,
With a nick-nack-paddy-wack,
Give the dog a bone,
This old man came rolling home.

4 This old man, he played FOUR,
He played nick-nack on my door,
With a nick-nack-paddy-wack,
Give the dog a bone,
This old man came rolling home.

5

This old man,
he played FIVE,

**He played nick-nack
on my hive,** With a
nick-nack-paddy-wack,
Give the dog a bone,
This old man came
rolling home.

This old man, he played SIX,

He played nick-nack on my sticks,
With a nick-nack-paddy-wack,
Give the dog a bone,
This old man came rolling home.

This old man, he played SEVEN,

He played nick-nack up in heaven,
With a nick-nack-paddy-wack,
Give the dog a bone,
This old man came rolling home.

This old man, he played EIGHT,

He played nick-nack on my gate,
With a nick-nack-paddy-wack,
Give the dog a bone,
This old man came rolling home.

This old man, he played NINE,

He played nick-nack on my spine,
With a nick-nack-paddy-wack,
Give the dog a bone,
This old man came rolling home.

This old man, he played TEN,

**When we're going home,
we can sing it again,**
With a nick-nack-paddy-wack,
Give the dog a bone,
This old man came rolling home.

Traditional. Adapted by Nancy Cassidy © 1986

CD 1/TRACK 17

The Fox

Oh, the fox went out on a **chilly night**,
Prayed for the moon to **give him light**,
He'd many a mile to go that night,
Before he reached the town-o, town-o, town-o,
He'd many a mile to go that night,
Before he reached the town-o.

He ran until he came to a **great big bin**,
The ducks and the geese **were kept therein**,
He said, "A couple of you are going to grease my chin,
Before I leave this town-o, town-o, town-o,"
He said, "A couple of you are going to grease my chin,
Before I leave this town-o."

He grabbed the grey goose **by the neck**,
Slung the little one **over his back**,
He didn't mind their "Quack! Quack! Quack!"
And the legs all dangling down-o, down-o down-o,
He didn't mind their "Quack! Quack! Quack!"
And the legs all dangling down-o.

Old Mother pitter patter **jumped out of bed**,
Out of the window she **cocked her head**,
Crying, "John, John, the grey goose is gone,
And the fox is on the town-o, town-o, town-o,"
Crying, "John, John, the grey goose is gone,
And the fox is on the town-o."

John he went to the **top of the hill**,
Blew his horn **both loud and shrill**,
The fox he said, "I better flee with my kill,
for he'll soon be on my trail-o, trail-o, trail-o,"
The fox he said, "I better flee with my kill,
For he'll soon be on my trail-o, trail-o."

He ran 'til he came to **his cozy den**,
There were the little ones, **eight**, **nine**, **ten**,
They said, "Daddy, Daddy, you better go back again,
for it must be a mighty fine town-o, town-o, town-o,"
They said, "Daddy, Daddy, you better go back again,
For it must be a mighty fine town-o."

Then the fox and his wife **without any strife**,
Cut up the goose with **a fork and a knife**,
They never had such a supper in their lives,
And the little ones chewed on
the bones-o, bones-o, bones-o,
They never had such a supper in their lives,
And the little ones chewed on the bones-o.

Traditional
CD 1/TRACK 18

Twinkle, Twinkle, Little Star

Twinkle,
twinkle little star,
How I wonder what you are,

Up above the world so high,
Like a diamond in the sky.

Twinkle, twinkle little star,
How I wonder what you are!

When I go to sleep at night,
Thanks for keeping me in sight,
Please keep watch upon the earth,
Keep us safe 'til morning light.

Twinkle, twinkle little star,
How I wonder what you are.

Traditional
Adapted by Nancy Cassidy © 1986

CD 1/TRACK 19

40

PUFF (the magic Dragon)

Puff!

Puff, the magic dragon, lived by the sea,

And frolicked in the **autumn mist**
in a land call Hanalee,

Little Jackie Paper **loved** that rascal Puff,

And brought him **strings** and **sealing wax**
and other **fancy stuff**.

CHORUS oh! Puff, the magic dragon, lived by the sea,

And frolicked in the autumn mist
in a land called Hanalee,

Puff, the magic dragon, lived by the sea,

And frolicked in
the autumn mist
in a land
called Hanalee.

Together they would travel on a boat
with billowed sail,

Jackie kept a lookout perched
on Puff's gigantic tail,

Noble kings and princes would
bow whene'er they came,

Pirate ships would
low'r their flag when
Puff roared out
his name.

Back to the chorus

A dragon lives forever but not so little boys,
Painted wings and giant rings make way for other toys,
One grey night it happened, Jackie Paper came no more,
And Puff that mighty dragon, he ceased his fearless roar.

His head was bent in sorrow, green scales fell like rain,
Puff no longer went to play along the cherry lane,
Without his lifelong friend, Puff could not be brave,
So Puff that mighty dragon sadly slipped into his cave.

Back to the chorus, repeat twice

CD 1/TRACK 20

43

Morningtown Ride

Train whistle blowing, makes a sleepy noise,
Underneath their blankets, go all the girls and boys,
Heading from the station, out along the bay,
All bound for Morningtown, many miles away.

Sarah's at the engine, Tony rings the bell,
Johnny swings a lantern, to show that all is well,
Rocking, rolling, riding, out along the bay,
All bound for Morningtown, many miles away.

Maybe it is raining, where our train will ride,
But all the little travelers
are snug and warm inside,
Somewhere there is sunshine,
somewhere there is day,
Somewhere there is Morningtown,
many miles away.

Words and music by Malvina Reynolds

CD 1/TRACK 21

This Little Light of mine

This little light of mine, I'm gonna let it shine,
This little light of mine, I'm gonna let it shine,
This little light of mine, I'm gonna let it shine,
Let it shine, let it shine, let it shine.

My brothers and my sisters, I'm gonna help them shine,
My brothers and my sisters, I'm gonna help them shine,
My brothers and my sisters, I'm gonna help them shine,
Help 'em shine, help 'em shine, help 'em shine.

This little love of ours, I'm gonna let it shine,
This little love of ours, I'm gonna let it shine,
This little love of ours, I'm gonna let it shine,
Let it shine, let it shine, let it shine.

This big world of ours, I'm gonna help it shine,
This big world of ours, I'm gonna help it shine,
This big world of ours, I'm gonna help it shine,
Help it shine, help it shine, help it shine.

Repeat first verse four times

Traditional. Adapted by Nancy Cassidy © 1986

CD 1 / TRACK 22

Have a Homemade
Jam Session!

Hollering along sounds even better with live accompaniment. Get a grown-up to help put together these whiz-bang instruments, round up some fellow musicians and rock out.

Humming Flute

materials empty paper towel roll, 4'' square of wax paper, tape, pencil

instructions With the pointy end of the pencil, poke three or four holes in the tube. Now fold the wax paper over one end of the tube. Securely tape it both to itself as well as to the tube. (This is important so the wax paper doesn't fly off the end when you put air in the tube.) To play it, place your mouth at the open end and hum into the tube.

materials two wooden spoons, big collection of pots and pans

instructions Clear out any grown-ups, turn the pots and pans upside down and bang away.

Kitchen Drums

Body Bells

materials as many jingle bells and shoelaces as you can get

instructions Tie three or four bells onto each shoelace and have someone tie each jingle bell lace around your wrists, ankles, waist, knee, toe, etc...then jiggle and jump!

Music Bottle

materials empty, dry small water or soda bottle with a cap, some dry macaroni noodles, glue

instructions Remove the cap from the bottle. Fill the bottle $\frac{1}{4}$ to $\frac{1}{2}$ full with the macaroni noodles. Place some glue on the inside edge of the cap and screw it back onto the bottle. When the glue dries, shake it like crazy.

Sand Blocks

materials two pieces of sandpaper, two hand-sized blocks of smooth wood, glue

instructions Glue the sandpaper to one side of the two pieces of wood. Then rub the two blocks together.

insert disc two

Kids Songs 2 KLUTZ

Play along with the next **22** songs!

She'll Be coming 'Round the mountain

She'll be coming 'round the mountain
when she comes. Toot! Toot!

She'll be coming 'round the mountain
when she comes. **Toot! Toot!**

She'll be coming 'round the mountain,
She'll be coming 'round the mountain,

She'll be coming 'round the mountain
when she comes. **Toot! Toot!**

★

She'll be driving six white horses
when she comes. whoa, back!

She'll be driving six white horses
when she comes. **Whoa, back!**

She'll be driving six white horses,
She'll be driving six white horses,

She'll be driving six white horses
when she comes. **Whoa, back!**

★

Oh, we'll all go out to meet her
when she comes. Hi, babe!

Oh, we'll all go out to meet her
when she comes. **Hi, babe!**

Oh, we'll all go out to meet her,

We'll all go out to meet her,

We'll all go out to meet her
when she comes. **Hi, babe!**

She'll be wearing red pajamas
when she comes. Scratch, scratch!

She'll be wearing red pajamas
when she comes. **Scratch, scratch!**

She'll be wearing red pajamas,

She'll be wearing red pajamas,

She'll be wearing red pajamas
when she comes. **Scratch, scratch!**

She will have to sleep with Grandma
when she comes. Snee, snore!

She will have to sleep with Grandma
when she comes. **Snee, snore!**

She will have to sleep with Grandma,

She'll have to sleep with Grandma,

She'll have to sleep with Grandma
when she comes. **Snee, snore!**

Scratch! Scratch! Hi Babe!
whoa, back! Toot! Toot!

Traditional
CD 2/TRACK 1

51

Sandwiches

CHORUS

Sandwiches are beautiful, sandwiches are fine,
I like sandwiches,
I eat them all the time.

I eat them for my supper and I eat them for my lunch.
If I had a hundred sandwiches,
I'd eat them all at once.

I'm **a-roamin'** and **a-travelin'** and **a-wanderin'** all along,
And if you care to listen, I will sing a happy song.
I will not **ask a favor** and I will not **ask a fee**,
But if you have a sandwich, **won't you give a bite to me?**

Back to the Chorus

Once I went to **England**, I visited the **Queen**,
I swear she was the grandest lady that I'd ever seen.
I told her **she was beautiful** and could not ask for more,
She handed me a sandwich and **threw me out the door**.

Back to the Chorus

A sandwich may be egg or cheese
or even peanut butter,

But they **all taste so good to me**,
it doesn't even matter.

Jam or ham or cucumber,
any kind will do.

Well, **I like sandwiches**,
how about you?

Back to the Chorus, repeat twice

CD 2/TRACK 2

RIG A JIG JIG

As I was walking down the street,
Down the street, down the street,
A very good friend I chanced to meet,
Hi Ho Hi Ho Hi Ho.

♪ CHORUS
Rig a jig jig and away we go, away we go, away we go,
Rig a jig jig and away we go, Hi Ho Hi Ho Hi Ho.

We clapped our hands and stomped our feet,
Stomped our feet, stomped our feet,
We clapped our hands and stomped our feet,
Hi Ho Hi Ho Hi Ho.

We jumped up high and came back down,
Came back down, came back down,
We jumped up high and came back down,
Hi Ho Hi Ho Hi Ho.
Back to the chorus

We climbed on a train and tooted the horn,
Tooted the horn, tooted the horn,
We climbed on a train and tooted the horn,
Hi Ho Hi Ho Hi Ho.

Kissed my ma and hugged my pa,
Hugged my pa, hugged my pa,
Kissed my ma and hugged my pa,
Hi Ho Hi Ho Hi Ho.
Back to the chorus

Traditional. Additional lyrics: Nancy Cassidy

CD 2/TRACK 3

55

Fooba-Wooba John

Saw a snail chase a whale, fooba-wooba, fooba-wooba.
Saw a snail chase a whale, Fooba-wooba John.
Saw a snail chase a whale, all around the water pail.
Hey, John, Ho, John, fooba-wooba John.

Saw a frog chase a dog, fooba-wooba, fooba-wooba.
Saw a frog chase a dog, Fooba-wooba John.
Saw a frog chase a dog, sitting on a hollow log.
Hey, John, Ho, John, fooba-wooba John.

Saw a flea kick a tree,
Fooba-wooba, fooba-wooba.

Saw a flea kick a tree,
Fooba-wooba John.

Saw a flea kick a tree,
in the middle of the sea.
Hey, John, Ho, John, Fooba-wooba John.

Heard a cow say "me-ow,"
Fooba-wooba, fooba-wooba.

Heard a cow say **"me-ow,"** Fooba-wooba John.
Heard a cow say **"me-ow,"** then I heard it
say, **"bow-wow."**

Hey, John, Ho, John, Fooba-wooba John.
Hey, John, Ho, John, Fooba-wooba John.

Traditional

CD 2 / TRACK 4

57

The Desperado

CHORUS For a bold bad man was this desperado,
From Badman's Gulch way down in Colorado.
And he rode around like a big tornado,
And ev'rywhere he went he gave his BIG whoop – Hey!

He was a desperado from the **wild and woolly West**,
But ev'ry now and then he'd go
and give the West a rest,
He saddled up his horse, put
on his **spurs and leather vest**,
And ev'rywhere he went he
gave his **BIG whoop — Hey!**
Back to the chorus

Hey!

He had a **skunk named Arnie**
but he thought he was a hat,
He'd put him **up on top his head**
and wear him just like that,
And ev'rywhere they'd go the
people'd point and say what's that,
And Arnie'd wag his tail and
give his **BIG whoop — HEY!**
Back to the chorus

Hey!

He had a **horse named Lightnin'**
but she wasn't very quick,
She never liked to run but she could
snort and buck and kick,
And when our desperado saddled up
and gave a kick,
She'd throw him so you'd really
hear his **BIG whoop — Hey!**
Back to the chorus

Traditional. Adapted by Nancy Cassidy © 1988

CD 2/TRACK 5

The BEEP! Bus Song
BEEP!   BEEP!

The wheels on the bus go round and round,
Round and round, round and round.
The wheels on the bus go round and round,
All through the town.

The wipers on the bus go, "Swish, swish, swish,"
"Swish, swish, swish, swish, swish, swish,"
The wipers on the bus go, "Swish, swish, swish,"
All through the town.

The horn on the bus goes, "Beep, beep, beep,"
"Beep, beep, beep, beep, beep, beep."
The horn on the bus goes, "Beep, beep, beep,"
All through the town.

The gas on the bus goes, "Glunk, glunk, glunk,"
"Glunk, glunk, glunk, glunk, glunk, glunk."
The gas on the bus goes, "Glunk, glunk, glunk,"
All through the town.

The money on the bus goes, "Clink, clink, clink,"
"Clink, clink, clink, clink, clink, clink."
The money on the bus goes, "Clink, clink, clink,"
All through the town.

The baby on the bus says, "Wah, wah, wah,"
"Wah, wah, wah, wah, wah, wah."
The baby on the bus says, "Wah, wah, wah,"
All through the town.

The mommy on the bus says,
"I love you, I love you, I love you."
The daddy on the bus says, "I love you, too."

All through the town. All through the town.
All through the town.

Traditional. Adapted by Nancy Cassidy © 1988

CD 2/TRACK 6

61

Lavender's Blue

Lavender's blue, dilly dilly, lavender's green,
When you are King, dilly dilly, I shall be Queen.
Who told you so, dilly dilly, who told you so?
'Twas my own heart, dilly dilly, that told me so.

Call up your friends, dilly dilly, set them to work.
Some to the plough, dilly dilly, some to the fork,
Some to the hay, dilly dilly, some to cut corn,
While you and I, dilly dilly, keep ourselves warm.

Lavender's blue, dilly dilly, lavender's green,
When you are King, dilly dilly, I shall be Queen.
Who told you so, dilly dilly, who told you so?
'Twas my own heart, dilly dilly, that told me so.

Traditional

CD 2/TRACK 7

There's a
Little Wheel
A-Turning

There's a little
wheel a-turning
in my heart,
There's a little
wheel a-turning
in my heart,
In my heart,
in my heart,
There's a **little wheel
a-turning** in my heart.

There's a little song a-singing in my heart,
There's a little song a-singing in my heart,
In my heart, in my heart,
There's a **little song a-singing** in my heart.

There's a little frog a-leaping in my heart,
There's a little frog a-leaping in my heart,
In my heart, in my heart,
There's a **little frog a-leaping** in my heart.

I see the sun a-rising in my heart,
I see the sun a-rising in my heart,
In my heart, in my heart,
I see the **sun a-rising** in my heart.

We're dancing 'round the world in my heart,
We're dancing 'round the world in my heart,
In my heart, in my heart,
We're **dancing 'round the world** in my heart.
Repeat first verse

Traditional. Adapted by Nancy Cassidy © 1988

CD 2/TRACK 8

ol' Texas

I'm going to leave ol' Texas now,
I'm going to leave ol' Texas now,

They've got no use for the long-horned cow.
They've got no use for the long-horned cow.

They've plowed and fenced my cattle range,
They've plowed and fenced my cattle range,

And the people there are all so strange.
And the people there are all so strange.

I'll take my horse, I'll take my rope,
I'll take my horse, I'll take my rope,

And hit the trail upon a lope.
And hit the trail upon a lope.

I'll bid adiós to the Alamo,
I'll bid adiós to the Alamo,

And turn my head toward Mexico.
And turn my head toward Mexico.

Traditional

CD 2/TRACK 9

Ghost Riders in

An old cowpoke went riding out one dark and windy day,
Upon a ridge he rested as he went along his way
When all at once a **mighty herd** of red-eyed cows he saw,
A-plowing through the **ragged skies**
and up a **cloudy draw**.
Yipee-yi-ay, Yipee-yi-oh, Ghost Riders in the sky.

Their brands were still on fire
and their hooves were made of steel,
Their horns were **black and shiny**
and their **hot breath** he could feel,

A **bolt of fear** went through him
as they **thundered through the sky**,

For he saw the **riders** coming hard
and heard their **mournful cry**.
Yipee-yi-ay, Yipee-yi-oh, Ghost Riders in the sky.

*Words and Music by Stan Jones © 1949 Edwin H. Morris & Company, A Division
of MPL Communications, Inc. © Renewed 1977 Edwin H. Morris & Company,
A Division of MPL Communications, Inc. International Copyright Secured.
All rights reserved. Used by permission.*

the Sky (A cowboy Legend)

Their faces gaunt, their eyes were blurred,
their shirts were soaked with sweat,

They're **riding hard** to catch that herd
but they ain't caught 'em yet.

They'll have to **ride forever** on that **range up in the sky**.

On horses breathing fire, **as they ride I hear them cry**,

Yipee-yi-ay, Yipee-yi-oh, Ghost Riders in the sky.

The riders loped on by him and
he heard one call his name,

"If you want to **save your hide**
and soul a-riding on this range,

Then cowboy, **change your ways** today
or **with us you will ride**,

Trying to catch the devil's herd
across the endless sky."

Yipee-yi-ay, Yipee-yi-oh, Ghost Riders in the sky.
Yipee-yi-ay, Yipee-yi-oh, Ghost Riders in the sky.

CD 2/ TRACK 10

Michael, Row the Boat Ashore

Michael, row the boat ashore, hallelujah,
Michael, row the boat ashore, hallelujah.

My brothers and sisters are all aboard, hallelujah,
My brothers and sisters are all aboard, hallelujah.
Michael, row the boat ashore, hallelujah,
Michael, row the boat ashore, hallelujah.

The river is deep and the river is wide, hallelujah,
Milk and honey on the other side, hallelujah.
Michael, row the boat ashore, hallelujah,
Michael, row the boat ashore, hallelujah.

Jordan's river is chilly and cold, hallelujah,
Chills the body but not the soul, hallelujah.
Michael, row the boat ashore, hallelujah,
Michael, row the boat ashore, hallelujah.

Michael, row the boat ashore, hallelujah,
Michael, row the boat ashore, hallelujah.

Traditional. Verse 1: Cody Cassidy

CD 2/ TRACK 11

La Bamba

Bamba bamba, bamba bamba, bamba bamba.
Para bailar la bamba, para bailar la bamba,
Se necesita una poca de gracia,
Una poca de gracia, y otra cosita,
Y arriba arriba, y arriba arriba,
y arriba arriba iré
Por ti seré, por ti seré.

Bamba bamba, bamba bamba, bamba bamba.
Let's dance with the music,
Let's dance with the music.
When we dance, we sing a song,
We sing a song of thanks,
And clap our hands and we go
faster and faster, higher and
higher, louder and louder.
Repeat first verse

Bamba bamba,
bamba bamba, bamba bamba,
Softer and softer – bamba la bamba – bamba!

Traditional. Adapted by Nancy Cassidy © 1988

CD 2/TRACK 12

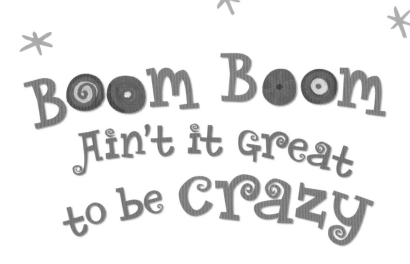

Boom Boom Ain't it great to be crazy

CHORUS
Boom, Boom ain't it great to be crazy,
Boom, Boom ain't it great to be crazy,
Giddy and foolish all day long,
Boom, Boom ain't it great to be crazy.

Way down South where bananas grow,
A flea stepped on an elephant's toe.
The elephant cried with tears in his eyes,
"Why don't you pick on someone your own size?"
Back to the chorus

Late last night I had a real strange dream,
Ate a nine pound marshmallow
momma gave me.
When I woke up I knew something was wrong,
I looked around, saw my pillow was gone.
Back to the chorus, repeat twice

Traditional. Adapted by Nancy Cassidy © 1988

CD 2/TRACK 13

Baa, baa, black sheep,
have you any wool?
Yes sir, yes sir, three bags full,
One for your **sweater**
and one for your **rug**,
And one for your **blanket**
to keep you **warm and snug**.

cluck, cluck
Red Hen

cluck, cluck red hen,
have you any eggs?
Yes sir, yes sir, as many as your legs,
One for your **breakfast** and one for your **lunch**,
Come back tomorrow
I'll have **another bunch**.

Moo, moo, brown cow,
have you milk for me?
Yes sir, yes sir, as tasty as can be,
Churn it into **butter**,
make it into **cheese**,
Freeze it into **ice cream**
or drink it **if you please**.

Buzz, buzz, busy bee, is your honey sweet?
Yes sir, yes sir, sweet enough to eat,
Honey on your **muffin**,
honey on your **cake**,
Honey by the spoonful,
as much as I can make.

Baa, baa, black sheep,
have you any wool?
Yes sir, yes sir,
three bags full.

CD 2/ TRACK 14

Hey Dum diddeley Dum

CHORUS

Hey dum diddeley dum,
Hey dum diddeley dum,
Hey dum diddeley, Hey dum diddeley,
Hey dum diddeley dum.

C'mon and sing along,
I've got the world's most singable song,
It's got a hey and a hum and a diddeley-dum,
And I hope you'll sing along.
Back to the chorus

It's kind of a help-along song,
It can help you out when
things go wrong.
When you're feeling sad,
and your day's gone bad,
Sing, hey dum diddeley dum.
Back to the chorus, repeat twice

Hey dum diddeley, Hey dum diddeley,
Hey dum diddeley dum.

Mark Stone. Additional lyrics: J. Cassidy.
© 1979 Pachyderm Music. Used by
permission. All rights reserved.
Adapted by Nancy Cassidy
© 1988

CD 2 / TRACK 15

The Old Chisholm Trail

Well, come along friends, listen to my tale,
I'll tell you my troubles on the old Chisholm trail.
Come-a ti yi yippy, yippy, yay, yippy yay!
Come-a ti yi yippy, yippy, yay!

On a ten-dollar horse, a forty-dollar saddle,
I started out a-punchin' those **long-horned cattle**.
Come-a ti yi yippy, yippy, yay, yippy yay!
Come-a ti yi yippy, yippy, yay!

I'm up in the morning before daylight,
Before I get to sleep the **moon's shining bright**.
Come-a ti yi yippy, yippy, yay, yippy yay!
Come-a ti yi yippy, yippy, yay!

It's **bacon and beans** 'most every day,
I'd sooner be eatin' the prairie hay.
Come-a ti yi yippy, yippy, yay, yippy yay!
Come-a ti yi yippy, yippy, yay!

I'll sell my outfit as soon as I can,
'Cause I ain't **punchin' cattle** for no mean boss man.
Come-a ti yi yippy, yippy, yay, yippy yay!
Come-a ti yi yippy, yippy, yay!

With **my knees in the saddle**, my seat in the sky,
I'll quit punchin' cattle in the sweet by an' by.
Come-a ti yi yippy, yippy, yay, yippy yay!
Come-a ti yi yippy, yippy, yay!

Come-a ti yi yippy, yippy, yay, yippy yay!
Come-a ti yi yippy, yippy, yay!

Traditional
CD 2/TRACK 16

My Dog Rags

I have a dog, his name is **Rags**,
He eats so much his **tummy sags**,
His ears flip flop, his **tail wig wags**,
And when he walks, he walks **zig zag**.

CHORUS
He goes flip flop, wig wag, zig zag,
He goes flip flop, wig wag, zig zag,
He goes flip flop, wig wag, zig zag,
I love Rags, and he loves me!

My dog Rags he loves to **play**,
He rolls around in the mud **all day**,
I whistle, he won't **obey**,
He always runs the other **way**.

Back to the chorus, repeat twice

CD 2/TRACK 17

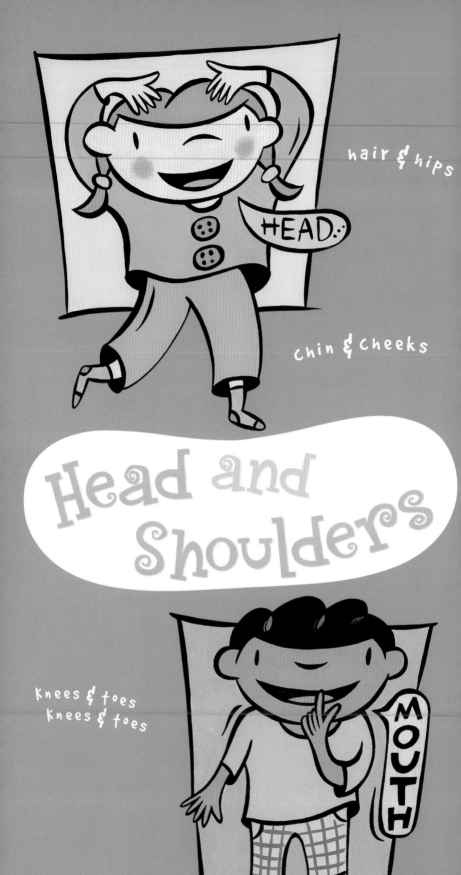

Head and shoulders, knees and toes, knees and toes.

Head and shoulders, knees and toes,
knees and toes,
And **eyes** and **ears** and **mouth** and **nose**,
Head and shoulders, knees and toes,
knees and toes.

Ankles, elbows, feet and seat, feet and seat.

Ankles, elbows, feet and seat,
and feet and seat,
And **hair** and **hips** and **chin** and **cheeks**,
Ankles, elbows, feet and seat,
feet and seat.

Repeat first verse, then second verse, then first verse again.

Traditional. Additional lyrics: Nancy & John Cassidy

CD 2/TRACK 18

He rocks in the treetops all day long,
Hoppin' and a-boppin' and **singin' his song**.
All the **little birdies** on J-Bird Street,
Love to hear the robin go **tweet, tweet, tweet**.

CHORUS

Rockin' robin
tweet, tweet, tweet,
Rockin' robin
tweet, tweedly-dee,
Go rockin' robin, we're
really gonna rock tonight.

Every little swallow, every chickadee,
Every little bird in the **tall oak tree**.
The **wise old owl**, the **big black crow**,
Flappin' their wings singin', **go bird, go**.
Back to the chorus

The **pretty little raven** and the **red-rock hen**,
Talkin' how the robin was **boppin' again**,
He started goin' steady and **"bless my soul,"**
He bopped out the **buzzard** and the **oriole**.

He rocks in the treetops all day long,
Hoppin' and a-boppin' and singin' his song.
All the little birdies on J-Bird Street,
Love to hear the robin go **tweet, tweet, tweet**.
Back to the chorus

Go ROCKIN' ROBIN, we're really gonna rock tonight.

CD 2/ TRACK 19

mail myself to you

I'm gonna wrap myself in paper,
I'm gonna daub myself with glue,
Stick some stamps on top
of my head,
I'm gonna mail myself to you.

Well, I'm gonna tie me up in a red string,
I'm gonna tie **blue ribbons** too,
I'm gonna climb up in my mailbox,
I'm gonna mail myself to you.

When you see me in your mailbox,
Cut the string and let me out,
Wash the glue off of my fingers,
Stick some **bubble gum** in my mouth.

Take me out of my wrapping paper,
Wash the stamps off my head,
Pour me full of **ice cream sodies**,
Put me in my nice warm bed.
Repeat first verse

*Words and music by Woody Guthrie. TRO — © Copyright 1962
(Renewed) 1963 (Renewed) Ludlow Music, Inc., New York, NY.
Used by permission.*

CD 2/ TRACK 20

Won't you bring back, won't you bring back,
Mrs. Murphy's chowder?

It was tuneful, ev'ry spoonful, made you YODEL louder.

After dinner Uncle Ben used to fill his fountain pen,

From a bowl of **Mrs. Murphy's chowder**.

CHORUS
There was ice cream, cold cream, benzine, gasoline,
Soup beans, string beans, floatin' all around.
Sponge cake, beef steak, mistake, stomach ache,
Cream puffs, ear muffs, many to be found.
Silk hats, door mats, bed slats, Democrats,
Cow bells, door bells, beckon you to dine.
Meat balls, fish balls, moth balls, cannon balls.
Come on in, the Chowder's fine!

Oh, won't you bring back, won't you bring back,
Mrs. Murphy's chowder?

It was tuneful, ev'ry spoonful, made you YODEL louder.

If they had it where you are, you might find a motor car,

In a bowl of **Mrs. Murphy's chowder**.

Back to the CHORUS

Traditional. Adapted by Nancy Cassidy © 1988

CD 2/ TRACK 21

He's Got the Whole World in his Hands

He's got the whole world in his hands,
He's got the whole world in his hands,
He's got the whole world in his hands,
He's got the **whole world** in his hands.

He's got my brothers and my sisters in his hands,
He's got my **brothers** and my **sisters** in his hands,
He's got my **brothers** and my **sisters** in his hands,
He's got the **whole world** in his hands.

He's got the sun and the rain in his hands,
He's got the **moon** and the **stars** in his hands,
He's got the **wind** and the **clouds** in his hands,
He's got the **whole world** in his hands.

He's got the rivers and the mountains in his hands,
He's got the **oceans** and the **seas** in his hands,
He's got **you** and he's got **me** in his hands,
He's got the **whole world** in his hands.

He's got everybody here in his hands,
He's got **everybody there** in his hands,
He's got **everybody everywhere** in his hands,
He's got the **whole world** in his hands.

Repeat first verse

Traditional. Adapted by Nancy Cassidy © 1988

CD 2/TRACK 22

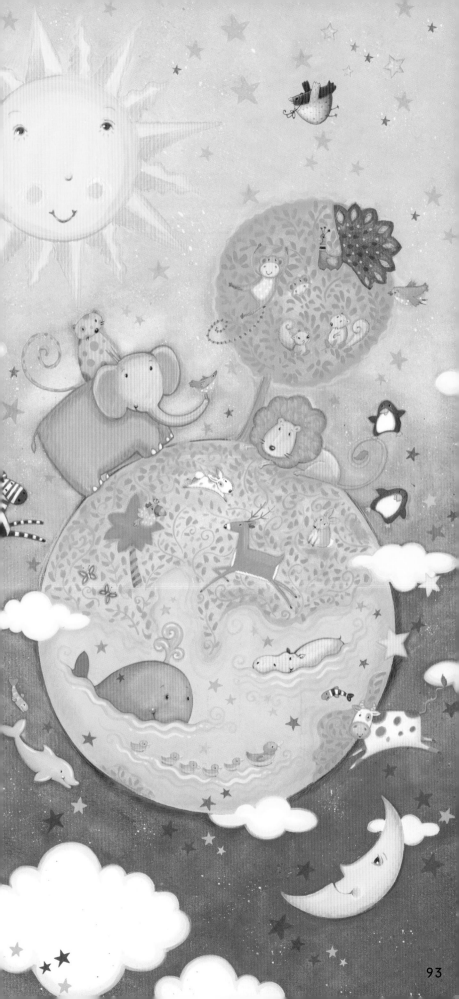

we'd like to say
thank you!

KidsSongs Disc 1 (originally released as **KidsSongs**) was recorded in May, 1986, in Toronto, Ontario at the Wellesley Sound Studios and at Casa Rossmore. It was produced by Ken Whiteley and engineered by Roger Slemin. The artists performing include these fine people:

Nancy Cassidy lead vocals, guitar

Ken Whiteley guitars (electric & acoustic), mandolin, synthesizer, piano, tambourine, jug, washboard, organ, accordian, washtub bass, triangle, high string guitar, banjo, autoharp, dobro, tenor banjo, kazoo, harmonica, rub board, slide guitar, mouth horn, Hawaiian guitar, train whistle.

Dennis Pendrith electric bass

Bucky Berger drums

Tom Szczesniak accordian

Dave Piltch string bass

Chris Whiteley harmonica, trumpet

Grit Laskin whistles, concertina, Appalachian dulcimer

Graham Townsend fiddle

Dick Smith conga, triangle, clave, pods, wood blocks

Earl Lapierre steel drums

Ron Dann pedal steel guitar

Jody Golick soprano saxophone

Mose Scarlett guitar, mouth horn

Caitlin Hanford mouth horn

Scott Irvine tuba

Sean Snell cymbals

The kids choir Cindy Tse, Valerie Shaugghnessy, Priya Glassey, Jamie Chiarelli, Mark & Damian Gryski, Toby Novorodsky, Erin Bentley, Andrew Fussner, Eden Fussner, Ben Penton, Zoe Campbell, Matty Chavel, Angus McClaren.

KidsSongs Disc 2 (originally released as **KidsSongs 2**) was recorded in May, 1988, in Toronto, Ontario, at the Wellesley Sound Studios and Maison Wroxton. It was produced by Ken Whiteley and engineered by Roger Slemin. Additional engineering by Bruce Cameron and Ken Whiteley. The artists featured in this recording:

Nancy Cassidy lead vocals

Ken Whiteley electric, acoustic and high string guitars, mandolin, synthesizer, piano, tambourine, organ, banjo, kazoo, percussion, dobro, autoharp and ukulele.

Dennis Pendrith electric bass

Bucky Berger drums, tympani